SURVIVE AN EARTHQUAKE

BY PATRICK PERISH

BELLWETHER MEDIA · MINNEAPOLIS, MN

Are you ready to take it to the extreme? Torque books thrust you into the action-packed world of sports, vehicles, mystery, and adventure. These books may include dirt, smoke, fire, and chilling tales. **WARNING** : read at your own risk.

This edition first published in 2017 by Bellwether Media, Inc.

No part of this publication may be reproduced in whole or in part without written permission of the publisher. For information regarding permission, write to Bellwether Media, Inc., Attention: Permissions Department, 5357 Penn Avenue South, Minneapolis, MN 55419.

Library of Congress Cataloging-in-Publication Data

Names: Perish, Patrick, author.
Title: Survive an Earthquake / by Patrick Perish.
Other titles: Survival Zone.
Description: Minneapolis, MN : Bellwether Media, Inc., 2017. | Series:
    Torque. Survival Zone | Includes bibliographical references and index.
    Audience: Ages 7-12. | Audience: Grades 3-7.
Identifiers: LCCN 2016035476 (print) | LCCN 2016039903 (ebook) | ISBN
    9781626175846 (hardcover : alk. paper) | ISBN 9781681033136 (ebook)
Subjects: LCSH: Survival–Juvenile literature. | Earthquakes–Juvenile
    literature. | Earthquake damage–Juvenile literature.
Classification: LCC QE521.3 .P465 2017 (print) | LCC QE521.3 (ebook) | DDC
    613.6/9–dc23
LC record available at https://lccn.loc.gov/2016035476

Editor: Christina Leaf   Designer: Jon Eppard

Printed in the United States of America, North Mankato, MN.

TABLE OF CONTENTS

EARTHQUAKE!

A 7.8 **magnitude** earthquake hit Kathmandu, Nepal, on April 25, 2015. When it began, 15-year-old Pemba Tamang was working at a hotel.

The powerful shaking began to crumble the walls. Suddenly, a concrete slab fell. When the dust settled, Pemba was trapped. A motorcycle had stopped the concrete from crushing him. But he could not stand up or stretch out. Stuck in his pocket of **rubble**, Pemba waited.

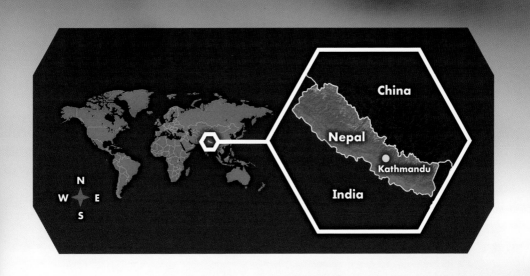

Kathmandu, Nepal

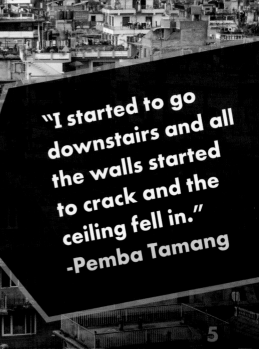

"I started to go downstairs and all the walls started to crack and the ceiling fell in."
-Pemba Tamang

5

Days passed. Pemba found a little water and ate some butter that he found in the rubble. Five days after the earthquake, he heard **excavators**. He shouted to the rescuers and threw rocks to alert them.

rescuers looking for Pemba

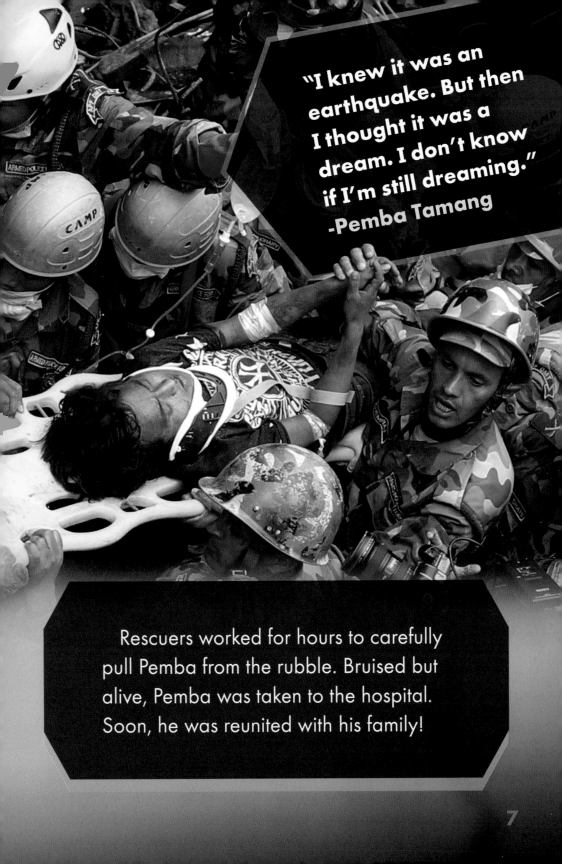

"I knew it was an earthquake. But then I thought it was a dream. I don't know if I'm still dreaming."
-Pemba Tamang

Rescuers worked for hours to carefully pull Pemba from the rubble. Bruised but alive, Pemba was taken to the hospital. Soon, he was reunited with his family!

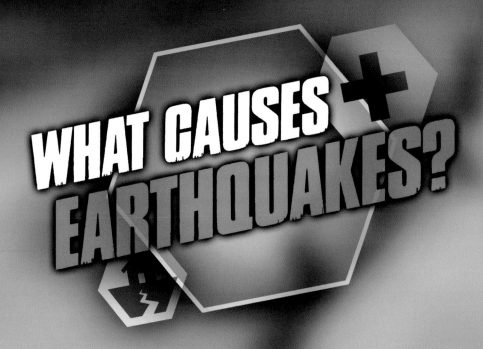

WHAT CAUSES EARTHQUAKES?

Earth's **crust** is broken up into pieces called **tectonic plates**. Humans do not feel it, but these plates are slowly moving. As they pass by one another, the plates get stuck. Pressure builds up. Suddenly, one piece slides by. Energy is released in powerful **seismic waves** moving outward from the **epicenter**. This is an earthquake.

PARTS OF AN EARTHQUAKE

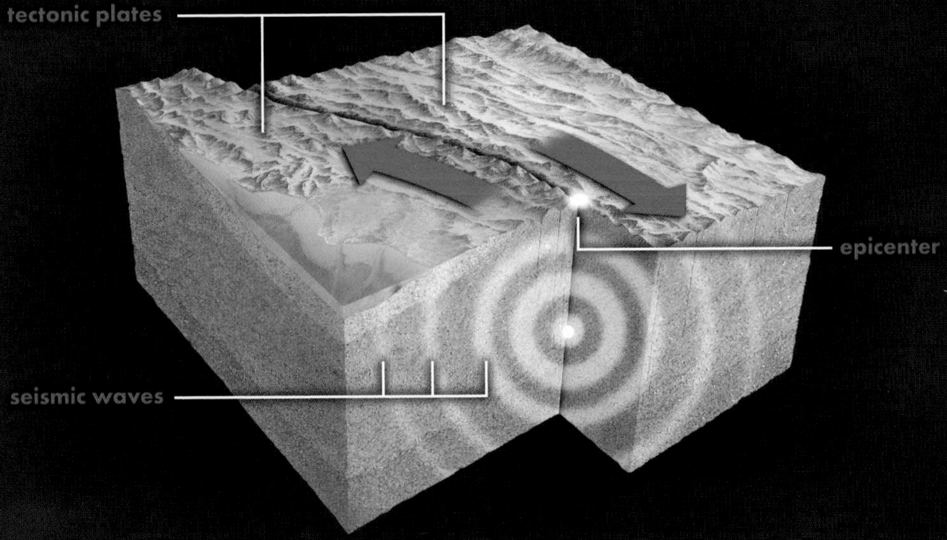

tectonic plates

epicenter

seismic waves

OTHER CAUSES

Earthquakes can also be set off by meteorites and volcanoes. Underground mining and drilling have caused quakes as well.

earthquake damage in Portoviejo, Ecuador

GETTING READY

Even with modern technology, scientists cannot predict earthquakes. Some places have early warning systems. But these only give people seconds to react.

The best way to protect yourself is to prepare. Check if you live in an area with regular earthquake activity. Most quakes happen along lines between plates, called **faults**.

TECTONIC PLATES

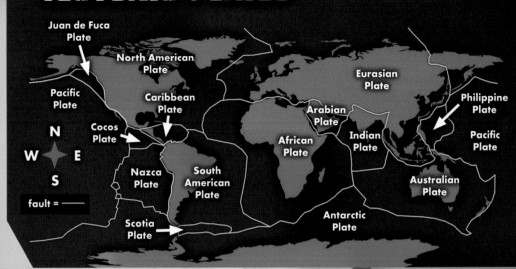

Juan de Fuca Plate

North American Plate

Pacific Plate

Caribbean Plate

Cocos Plate

Eurasian Plate

Arabian Plate

Philippine Plate

Indian Plate

African Plate

Pacific Plate

Nazca Plate

South American Plate

Australian Plate

N
W   E
S

Scotia Plate

Antarctic Plate

fault = ⎯⎯⎯

CLEVER CRITTERS

Some people believe animals may be able to predict earthquakes. Rats, toads, dogs, and other animals have been known to behave strangely right before a quake.

WILD WATERS

In 1811 and 1812, powerful earthquakes struck near the Arkansas and Missouri border. The shifting ground caused the Mississippi River to flow backward.

Do your best to prepare your home. Heavy furniture like bookshelves can be bolted to the wall. Use putty or Velcro to keep smaller objects from falling and causing damage.

Identify places in your home or school where you could take cover. Practice so the action is familiar. Make an emergency plan with your family. Know where to meet up or leave messages if you get separated.

DURING THE QUAKE

During a quake you must act quickly. Get down on the ground to avoid falling. Protect your head and neck by taking cover and shielding them with an arm. Falling **debris** can be deadly.

Get under sturdy furniture and hold on until the shaking stops. Keep away from windows. If you are outside, stay far from tall structures that may **collapse**, like trees or buildings.

EARTHQUAKE SAFETY

Drop, Cover, and Hold On is the best way to stay safe during an earthquake. Be sure to practice so you are ready if an earthquake hits.

DROP

COVER

HOLD ON

rescuers after 2014 earthquake, Yunnan province, China

If you find yourself trapped, do not panic. Breathing may be difficult. Avoid kicking dust and dirt up into the air.

Try to call for help. Use a cell phone if you have one. Banging on metal or whistling may help signal to rescuers.

A LOT OF SHAKING

Machines detect about 500,000 earthquakes each year. Around 100,000 are noticeable but only about 100 do damage.

AFTER THE QUAKE

When the earthquake stops, find a safe way outside. Locate an open area away from damaged objects and buildings. Be ready for **aftershocks**. They may hit the area days, weeks, or even months later.

Before reentering a building, make sure an adult says it is safe. Walls may be damaged. Objects inside cupboards and closets may have moved and could fall out.

MEASURING EARTHQUAKES

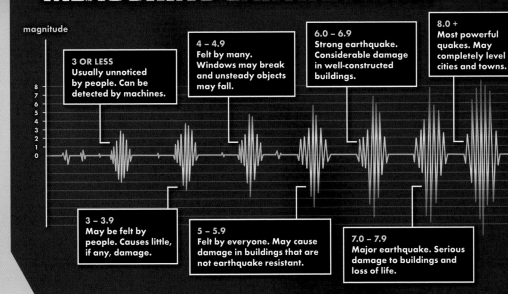

magnitude

3 OR LESS
Usually unnoticed by people. Can be detected by machines.

4 – 4.9
Felt by many. Windows may break and unsteady objects may fall.

6.0 – 6.9
Strong earthquake. Considerable damage in well-constructed buildings.

8.0 +
Most powerful quakes. May completely level cities and towns.

3 – 3.9
May be felt by people. Causes little, if any, damage.

5 – 5.9
Felt by everyone. May cause damage in buildings that are not earthquake resistant.

7.0 – 7.9
Major earthquake. Serious damage to buildings and loss of life.

BETTER BUILDINGS

Scientists have designed buildings that can withstand moderate earthquakes. They sway with the quake but do not collapse.

19

Listen to local news reports for emergency information and instructions. Gas pipes may be leaking and in danger of exploding. Stay away from downed power lines.

2011 Japan tsunami

テレトラック
MIYAKO

DANGERS CONTINUE

Earthquakes often cause other disasters. Tsunamis, fires, avalanches, and mudslides can all be set off by earthquakes.

EARTHQUAKE HOT SPOTS

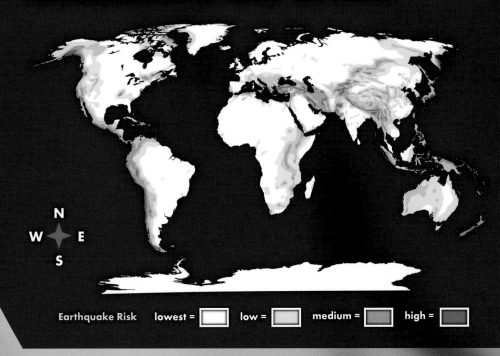

N
W ✦ E
S

Earthquake Risk lowest = ▢ low = ▢ medium = ▢ high = ▢

Authorities may order an **evacuation** of a badly damaged area. It can take years for a disaster area to return to normal. Prepare and practice as much as you can. Then you will be ready if an earthquake hits!

GLOSSARY

aftershocks—smaller earthquakes that follow a
large earthquake

collapse—to fall apart

crust—the outermost layer of Earth

debris—the remains of something broken down or destroyed

epicenter—the part of Earth's surface right above where an
earthquake begins

evacuation—the process of leaving a dangerous area

excavators—large machines used for clearing debris
and digging

faults—the breaks in Earth's crust that separate tectonic plates

identify—to find and know what something is

magnitude—the power of an earthquake

rubble—broken pieces of brick, stone, or other materials from a
fallen building

seismic waves—waves of energy in the ground or along its
surface caused by earthquakes

tectonic plates—the layers of Earth's crust that move

AT THE LIBRARY

Brooks, Susie. *Earthquakes and Volcanoes*. New York, N.Y.: PowerKids Press, 2016.

Hanel, Rachael. *Can You Survive an Earthquake?: An Interactive Survival Adventure*. North Mankato, Minn.: Capstone Press, 2013.

Hoobler, Dorothy and Thomas. *What Was the San Francisco Earthquake?* New York, N.Y.: Grosset & Dunlap, 2016.

ON THE WEB

Learning more about surviving an earthquake is as easy as 1, 2, 3.

1. Go to www.factsurfer.com.

2. Enter "survive an earthquake" into the search box.

3. Click the "Surf" button and you will see a list of related web sites.

With factsurfer.com, finding more information is just a click away.

INDEX